Christmas Treat Recipes

Hannie P. Scott

www.HanniePScott.com

www.Hanniepscott.com

ISBN: 9781973497349

MY FREE GIFT TO YOU!

55
Quick
&
Easy
Recipes

hannie p. scott

To download your free gift, simply visit:

www.hanniepscott.com/freegift

TABLE OF CONTENTS

For more books by Hannie, please visit:
www.Hanniepscott.com/books

ABBREVIATIONS

oz = ounce

fl oz = fluid ounce

tsp = teaspoon

tbsp = tablespoon

ml = milliliter

c = cup

pt = pint

qt = quart

gal = gallon

L = liter

CONVERSIONS

1/2 fl oz = 3 tsp = 1 tbsp = 15 ml

1 fl oz = 2 tbsp = 1/8 c = 30 ml

2 fl oz = 4 tbsp = 1/4 c = 60 ml

4 fl oz = 8 tbsp = 1/2 c = 118 ml

8 fl oz = 16 tbsp = 1 c = 236 ml

16 fl oz = 1 pt = 1/2 qt = 2 c = 473 ml

128 fl oz = 8 pt = 4 qt = 1 gal = 3.78 L

FUDGE

candy cane Fudge

Makes 36 squares

What you need:

- 3 cups white chocolate chips
- 1 14-oz can sweetened condensed milk
- 1 tsp vanilla extract
- 8 crushed candy canes

What to do:

1. Line a 9x9-inch baking dish with parchment paper and grease it.
2. In a large saucepan, combine the white chocolate chips and sweetened condensed milk. Continue stirring until all of the white chocolate chips have completely melted.
3. Stir in the vanilla extract and the crushed candy canes.
4. Transfer to the prepared baking dish and allow it to cool for about an hour.
5. Place the baking dish in the refrigerator and allow it to set for an additional 3-4 hours.

Fudge

Servings: 8-10

What you need:

- 1 cup dark chocolate chips
- 1 cup of coconut milk
- 1/4 cup of honey

What to do:

1. Mix the ingredients directly into your slow cooker.
2. Cook on low for 2 hours.
3. Stir until the mixture is smooth.
4. Pour the fudge mixture into a greased casserole dish.
5. Cover the fudge with plastic wrap and refrigerate for at least 3 hours before serving.

Old Fashioned Chocolate Fudge

Makes 36 squares

What you need:

- 2 cups white sugar
- 1/2 cup cocoa
- 1 cup milk
- 4 tbsp butter
- 1 tsp vanilla extract

What to do:

1. Line a 9x9-inch square baking pan with parchment paper and grease.
2. In a medium saucepan, combine the sugar, cocoa, and milk. Stir to mix together well and bring it to a boil while constantly stirring. Reduce heat to low.
3. Cook, without stirring, until a candy thermometer reaches 238 degrees F.
4. Remove from the heat. Add in the butter and vanilla extract. Stir very well with a wooden spoon.
5. Pour the fudge into the prepared pan and let cool for one hour.
6. Place the baking pan in the refrigerator and let set for 3-4 hours.

peppermint crunch Fudge

Servings: 20

What you need:

- 1 bag peppermint Hershey's Kisses, unwrapped and chopped
- 1/2 cup Andes Peppermint Crunch bites
- 1 cup sugar
- 1/2 cup heavy cream
- 1/2 tsp salt
- 1/2 cup butter
- 1 bag white chocolate chips
- 7-oz marshmallow fluff

What to do:

1. Line a 9x9-inch baking dish with parchment paper.
2. In a large saucepan over medium heat, melt together the sugar, heavy cream, salt, and butter. Bring it to a boil and cook for 5 minutes.
3. Place the white chocolate chips and marshmallow fluff in a large glass bowl.
4. Pour the boiling sugar mixture into the bowl with the chocolate chips and marshmallow fluff and mix with a mixer until smooth.
5. Fold in 3/4 of the chopped Kisses.
6. Pour the mixture into the prepared pan.
7. Sprinkle the rest of the kisses and the Andes Bits on top of the fudge.

8. Refrigerate for a couple hours or until set.
9. Cut into squares and serve or store in an airtight container.

Red Velvet Fudge

Makes 24 squares

What you need:

- 3 cups sugar
- 3/4 cup butter
- 2/3 cup half and half
- 12-oz white chocolate chips
- 7-oz marshmallow cream
- 1 tsp vanilla
- 1 cup semi-sweet chocolate chips
- 3 tbsp red food coloring

What to do:

1. Line a 9x9-inch baking dish with foil, with the ends of the foil extending over the sides. Lightly spray the foil with non-stick spray.
2. In a large glass microwave safe bowl, add the butter and cover with a paper towel. Microwave on high for 1 1/2 minutes.
3. Add the sugar and the half and half to the melted butter and mix well. Microwave for 3 minutes. Stir and cook for another 2 minutes.
4. Stir very well, scrape down the sides, and microwave for another 2 minutes.
5. Add the marshmallow cream and stir.
6. Add the white chocolate chips and vanilla. Stir until everything is very smooth.

7. In a separate microwave bowl, add the semi-sweet chocolate chips and food coloring. Add half of the hot white chocolate mixture into the bowl with the semi-sweet chocolate chips. Stir well.

8. With 2 ice cream scoops, dollop scoops of each mixture into a random pattern into the prepared baking dish.

9. When all of both of the mixtures are in the pan, lift the pan about an inch and drop it on the counter to remove air bubbles. Repeat about 5 times.

10. Run a knife through the fudge mixture to make it swirly.

11. Let the fudge cool completely before lifting it from the dish and cutting into squares.

White Chocolate Peppermint Fudge

Makes 2 lbs

What you need:

- 1 1/2 tsp plus 1/4 cup butter, softened
- 2 cups sugar
- 1/2 cup sour cream
- 12-oz white chocolate baking squares, chopped
- 7-oz marshmallow cream
- 1/2 cup crushed peppermints
- 1/2 tsp peppermint extract

What to do:

1. Line a 9x9-inch baking dish with foil. Grease the foil with 1 1/2 tsp of butter.
2. In a large heavy saucepan over medium heat, combine the sugar, sour cream, and 1/4 cup butter. Stir until the sugar is dissolved then bring to a rapid boil. Stir until a candy thermometer reaches 234 degrees F (about 5 minutes).
3. Remove the saucepan from the heat and stir in the white chocolate and marshmallow cream until they are melted.
4. Fold in the crushed peppermints and peppermint extract.
5. Pour the mixture into the prepared pan.
6. Place the pan in your refrigerator for at least an hour or until firm.

7. Lift the fudge out of the pan and gently peel off the foil.
8. Cut into 1-inch squares.

COOKIES AND BROWNIES

Butterfinger Cookies

Makes 2 1/2 dozen

What you need:

- 1 3/4 cups all-purpose flour
- 3/4 tsp baking soda
- 1/4 tsp salt
- 3/4 cup granulated sugar
- 1/2 cup butter, softened
- 1 large egg
- 8 fun sized Butterfingers, chopped

What to do:

1. Preheat your oven to 350 degrees F.
2. In a mixing bowl, combine the flour, baking soda, and salt. Set aside.
3. In a separate mixing bowl, beat the sugar and butter with an electric mixer until creamy then mix in the egg.
4. Slowly mix in the flour mixture.
5. Stir in the Butterfinger pieces with a spoon.
6. Drop tablespoonfuls of dough onto prepared baking sheet 2 inches apart.
7. Bake for 10-12 minutes or until lightly golden.
8. Allow the cookies to cool for 5 minutes then transfer them to a wire rack to cool completely.

cake Batter christmas cookies

Makes 2 dozen

What you need:

- · 1 1/4 cups all-purpose flour
- · 1 1/4 cup yellow boxed cake mix
- · 1/2 tsp baking soda
- · 3/4 cup butter, softened
- · 1/2 cup sugar
- · 1/2 cup brown sugar
- · 1 egg
- · 1 1/2 tsp vanilla extract
- · 1 cup white chocolate chips
- · 1/2 cup Christmas colored sprinkles

What to do:

1. In a large bowl, sift together the flour, cake mix, and baking soda.
2. In another large bowl, mix together (with a hand mixer) the butter and both sugars until smooth.
3. Add in the egg and mix for 1 minute until combined. Scrape down the sides of the bowl as needed.
4. Add the vanilla and mix until combined.
5. Add the flour mixture a little bit at a time at low speed until all of it is mixed in well.

6. Mix in the chocolate chips and sprinkles on low speed.
7. Cover and refrigerate the dough for at least 2 hours.
8. Preheat your oven to 350 degrees F and line 2 large baking sheets with parchment paper.
9. Form the dough into balls about 1 and a half tbsp each. Make the balls taller than they are round to make thicker cookies.
10. Bake the cookies for 10-12 minutes or until the edges are browned.
11. Allow the cookies to cool for 5 minutes on the baking sheet for 5 minutes then transfer them to a wire rack to cool completely.

Chocolate Caramel Cookies

Makes 2 1/2 dozen

What you need:

- 1 package devil's food cake mix
- 2 eggs
- 1/2 cup canola oil
- 42 Rolo candies
- Christmas colored M&M's

What to do:

1. Preheat your oven to 350 degrees F and line 2 baking sheets with parchment paper.
2. In a large bowl, mix together the cake mix, eggs, and oil.
3. Roll the dough into tbsp sized balls and place 1-2 inches apart on the prepared baking sheets.
4. Press a Rolo into each ball.
5. Bake for 8-10 minutes.
6. As soon as you remove the cookies from the oven, press 4 M&M's onto each cookie.
7. Let cool and serve!

Chocolate Peppermint Cookies

Servings: 15

What you need:

- 3/4 cup butter, softened
- 1/2 cup brown sugar, packed
- 1/2 cup sugar
- 1 egg
- 1/2 tsp vanilla extract
- 1/2 tsp peppermint extract
- 1 1/4 cups all-purpose flour
- 1/2 cup cocoa
- 1 tsp baking soda
- 1/2 cup Andes Peppermint Crunch pieces
- 3/4 cup chopped Oreos

What to do:

1. In a mixing bowl, cream together the butter and sugar until light and fluffy.
2. Mix in the egg and vanilla extract.
3. In a separate bowl, whisk together the flour, cocoa, and baking powder until combined.
4. Gradually add the flour mixture to the butter and sugar mixture and mix until combined well.
5. Cover and refrigerate for at least an hour.

6. Preheat your oven to 350 degrees F and line a baking sheet with parchment paper.

7. Form the dough into 1 to 2-inch balls and place them on the baking sheet 1 inch apart.

8. Bake for 8-10 minutes or until the edges look firm. The middle should still look soft.

9. Remove from the oven and cool for 2 minutes before transferring to a wire rack to cool completely.

christmas cookies

Makes 2 dozen

What you need:

- 1 roll of sugar cookie dough
- 1 cup powdered sugar
- 1/2 tsp vanilla extract
- 2 tbsp milk
- Christmas colored food coloring
- 1 cup powdered sugar
- 1/2 tsp vanilla extract
- 2 1/2 tbsp milk
- 2 small tipped squeeze bottles
- Christmas cookie cutters

What to do:

1. Preheat your oven to 350 degrees F.
2. On a large sheet of wax paper, roll out the sugar cookie dough to about 1/4-inch thickness with a rolling pin.
3. Cut shapes out of the cookie dough and bake according to package directions. I used a snowflake cookie cutter.
4. Once the cookies are completely cooled, return them to the wax paper on your counter.
5. First, prepare a thicker icing for the border of the cookies. Mix together 1 cup powdered sugar, 1/2 tsp vanilla, and 2 tbsp of milk in a small bowl. You can add food coloring if you would like, I chose to keep the thicker icing white. Place a funnel in

the mouth of one of the squeeze bottles and funnel the icing into it. The icing should be thick enough to just barely pour out. You may need to add another teaspoon or 2 of milk.

6. Next, prepare the filler icing. Mix together 1 cup powdered sugar, 1/2 tsp vanilla, and 2 1/2 tbsp of milk in a small bowl. Add food coloring if you would like. I used red. You could divide the icing in half or quarters and make multiple colors (make more icing if needed). Transfer the icing into a different squeeze bottle using a clean funnel. The filler icing should be thinner, add a teaspoon or 2 of milk if it isn't thin enough for your liking.

7. Decorate the borders of your cookies with the thicker icing and let the icing dry almost completely before decorating with the filler icing.

8. Decorate with the filler icing and let the icing dry completely before serving the cookies.

Eggnog Cookies

Makes about 32 cookies

What you need:

-Cookies:

- 2 1/4 cups all-purpose flour
- 2 tsp baking powder
- 1/2 tsp salt
- 1/2 tsp ground nutmeg
- 1/2 tsp ground cinnamon
- 3/4 cup butter, at room temperature
- 1/2 cup sugar
- 1/2 cup brown sugar
- 2 large egg yolks
- 1 tsp vanilla extract
- 1/2 tsp rum extract
- 1/2 cup eggnog

-Frosting:

- 1/2 cup butter
- 3-5 tbsp eggnog
- 1/2 tsp rum extract
- 3 cups powdered sugar

What to do:

1. Preheat your oven to 350 degrees F and line 2 baking sheets with parchment paper.

2. In a mixing bowl, whisk together the flour, baking powder, salt, nutmeg, and cinnamon. Set aside.
3. In a separate mixing bowl, cream together the butter, sugar, and brown sugar until fluffy with an electric mixer.
4. Mix in the egg yolks, one at a time, until just combined.
5. Mix in the vanilla extract, rum extract, and eggnog.
6. Slowly add the dry ingredients to the wet ingredients and mix on low until combined.
7. Scoop tablespoonfuls onto the prepared baking sheets, 2 inches apart.
8. Bake for 11-13 minutes.
9. Let cool on the baking sheets for 5 minutes before transferring to a wire rack to cool completely.
10. For frosting, whip the butter, rum extract, and 3 tbsp eggnog together. Gradually add the powdered sugar. Add additional eggnog until the frosting is desired consistency.
11. Frost the cooled cookies before serving.

Gingerbread Cookies

Makes 24 cookies

What you need:

- 1/2 cup butter, softened
- 1/2 cup butter flavored shortening
- 1 1/2 cups sugar
- 1 egg
- 1 tbsp vanilla
- 3 tbsp molasses
- 3 cups all-purpose flour
- 2 tbsp baking soda
- 2 tsp ground cinnamon
- 1 tsp ground ginger
- 1/2 tsp ground cloves
- 1/2 tsp salt
- Frosting

What to do:

1. In a large mixing bowl, cream together the butter, shortening, and sugar. Add in the egg, vanilla and molasses and mix well.

2. In a separate bowl, whisk together the flour, baking soda, cinnamon, ginger, ground cloves, and salt.
3. Add the flour mixture to the butter mixture a little bit at a time until it is all mixed in well. It will be thick!
4. Cover and refrigerate the dough for at least 2 hours.

5. Preheat your oven to 375 degrees F.
6. Lightly flour a large cutting board or sheet of wax paper.
7. Roll the dough on the floured surface and roll out into a sheet 1/4-inch thick.
8. Using a gingerbread man (or whatever shape you want!) cookie cutter, cut the dough.
9. Place the cut dough onto a greased baking sheet.
10. Bake for 10-12 minutes.
11. Let the cookies cool then decorate them with frosting.

Grinch Cookies

Makes about 3 dozen

What you need:

- 1 box French vanilla cake mix
- 1/2 cup vegetable oil
- 2 eggs
- 2 drops green food coloring
- Powdered sugar
- Red heart shaped candies

What to do:

1. Preheat your oven to 350 degrees F and line a baking sheet or two with parchment paper.
2. In a large mixing bowl, mix together the cake mix, food coloring, oil, and eggs with an electric mixer.
3. Chill the dough for 30 minutes.
4. Roll the dough into 1-inch balls and place on the prepared baking sheet 1-2 inches apart.
5. Dust each cookie dough ball with powdered sugar and place a heart-shaped candy in the center of each.
6. Bake for 8-9 minutes then let cool on the baking sheets for 5 minutes before transferring to a wire rack to cool completely.
7. Serve or store in an airtight container.

Hot Chocolate Cookies

Makes 1 dozen

What you need:

- 1 roll of chocolate chip cookie dough, at room temperature
- 1 cup Nutella
- 3 tbsp unsweetened cocoa powder
- 3/4 tsp ground cinnamon
- 6 large marshmallows, cut in half

What to do:

1. Preheat your oven to 350 degrees F and line two baking sheets with parchment paper.
2. In a large bowl, break up the cookie dough and add the Nutella, cocoa powder, and cinnamon.
3. Beat with an electric mixer until well mixed.
4. Shape the dough into 12 2-inch balls. Flatten the balls and place half of a large marshmallow in the center of each and fold the dough around the marshmallow.
5. Place the balls 2-inches apart on the baking sheets and bake for 10-12 minutes.
6. Cool on the pan for 5 minutes then transfer to a rack to cool completely before serving.

M&M Cookies

Makes 2 1/2 dozen

What you need:

· 2 1/2 cups all-purpose flour
· 2 tsp cornstarch
· 3/4 tsp baking powder
· 1/2 tsp baking soda
· 1 cup butter
· 1 cup brown sugar
· 1/2 cup white sugar
· 1 large egg
· 2 tsp vanilla extract
· 1 11-oz bag M&M's

What to do:

1. Preheat your oven to 375 degrees F and line 2 baking sheets with parchment paper.
2. In a mixing bowl, whisk together the flour, cornstarch, baking powder, baking soda, and salt. Set aside.
3. In a separate mixing bowl, mix together the butter and sugar with an electric mixer until creamy.
4. Mix in the egg and the additional egg yolk.
5. Mix in the vanilla.
6. Slowly mix in the flour mixture until combined.
7. Stir in the M&M's with a spoon, reserve 1/4 cup of M&M's for the tops of the cookies.

8. Scoop out 2 tbsp of dough at a time and form into a balls then place on the prepared baking sheet 2 inches apart.
9. Bake for 10-12 minutes until the edges are golden.
10. Allow the cookies to cool on the baking sheet for 5 minutes then transfer to a wire rack to cool completely.

oreo peppermint cookies

Makes 36 cookies

What you need:

- 1 box white cake mix
- 1 stick butter, melted
- 1 egg
- 1/2 tsp peppermint extract
- 1/2 tsp vanilla extract
- 4-oz cream cheese, softened and cubed
- 1 cup crushed Oreos
- 1 cup Andes Peppermint Crunch pieces
- 1/2 cup chocolate chips

What to do:

1. In a mixing bowl, combine the cake mix, melted butter, egg, peppermint extract, and vanilla extract. Beat until a dough forms.
2. Add the cream cheese to the dough and mix until combined.
3. Stir in the peppermint crunch pieces and chocolate chips.
4. Stir in the crushed Oreos gently.
5. Refrigerate the dough for 30 minutes.
6. Preheat your oven to 350 degrees F and line a baking sheet or two with parchment paper and spray with non-stick spray.
7. Roll the dough into balls and line them 1-inch apart on the prepared pans.
8. Bake for 9-10 minutes.

9. Remove the pans from the oven and let the cookies sit for 2 minutes before transferring to a wire rack or a sheet of wax paper to cool completely.

peppermint Brownies

Servings: 8-10

What you need:

- Your favorite boxed brownie mix plus ingredients the directions call for
- 1/2 cup green and red chocolate morsels
- 8-oz cream cheese
- 1/3 cup butter, softened
- 1/2 cup powdered sugar
- 12 peppermint Hershey's Kisses, chopped
- 1/4 tsp peppermint extract
- 3 candy canes, crushed
- Chocolate sauce

What to do:

1. Mix together your brownie mix according to box directions and stir in the 1/2 cup green and red chocolate morsels.
2. While the brownies are baking and cooling, beat the cream cheese and butter in a large bowl with a mixer until creamy and smooth.
3. Gradually add the powdered sugar and mix until smooth.
4. Mix in the peppermint extract.
5. Stir in the chopped Hershey's Kisses.
6. Spread the frosting over the cooled brownies.
7. Sprinkle the crushed candy canes over the frosting.
8. Drizzle on the chocolate sauce.

9. Cut into squares and serve.

peppermint cookies

Makes 3 dozen

What you need:

· 1 1/2 cups powdered sugar
· 1 cup butter, softened
· 1 tsp peppermint extract
· 1 tsp vanilla extract
· 1 egg
· 3 cups flour
· 3 candy canes, crushed
· 1 tsp baking powder
· 1 tsp salt
· 1/2 cup chopped peppermint Hershey's Kisses
· Sugar
· 36 peppermint Hershey's Kisses

What to do:

1. Preheat you oven to 350 degrees F.

2. Line 2 baking sheets with parchment paper and spray with non-stick spray.

3. In a large bowl, mix the powdered sugar, butter, vanilla extract, peppermint extract, and egg with an electric mixer until fluffy.

4. In a separate bowl, combine the flour, crushed candy canes, baking powder, and salt.

5. Add the flour mixture to the wet mixture and mix until well blended.
6. Stir in the chopped Hershey's Kisses.
7. Place about 1/4 cup – 1/2 cup of sugar in a small bowl.
8. Shape the dough into 1-inch balls and roll into the sugar.
9. Place the dough balls on the prepared baking sheets 1-inch apart.
10. Bake for 10-12 minutes or until set.
11. Remove the cookies from the oven and let them cool for 5 minutes then press a Hershey's Kiss in the center of each cookie.

peppermint kiss cookies

Makes: 2 1/2 dozen

What you need:

· 1 1/2 cups powdered sugar
· 1 1/4 cups butter, softened
· 1 tsp peppermint extract
· 1 tsp vanilla extract
· 1 large egg
· 3 cups all-purpose flour
· 1 tsp baking powder
· 1/2 tsp salt
· 1/2 cup finely chopped candy cane flavored Hershey's Kisses
· Granulated sugar
· Additional unwrapped Candy Cane Hershey's Kisses

What to do:

1. Preheat your oven to 350 degrees F and line a baking sheet with parchment paper.

2. In a mixing bowl, mix together the powdered sugar, butter, peppermint extract, vanilla extract, and egg with an electric mixer until creamy.

3. In a separate bowl, whisk together the flour, baking powder, and salt.

4. Slowly add the flour mixture to the sugar/butter mixture until combined.

5. Stir in the chopped Kisses with a spoon.
6. Shape the dough into 1-inch balls and roll in granulated sugar. Place the balls 1-inch apart on the prepared sheet.
7. Bake for 10-12 minutes or until slightly golden.
8. Let the cookies cool for 2-3 minutes on the baking sheet then press a Hershey's Kiss into each cookie.
9. Place the baking sheet in the refrigerator or freezer immediately so that the Kisses don't melt. Leave them in there for 5-10 minutes.
10. Serve or store in an airtight container.

Red Velvet Cookies

Makes 2 dozen

What you need:

- 1 box red velvet cake mix
- 6 tbsp butter, melted
- 1 cup powdered sugar
- 1 tsp cornstarch
- 2 eggs

What to do:

1. Preheat your oven to 375 degrees F and line a baking sheet with parchment paper.
2. Combine the cornstarch and powdered sugar in a small bowl.
3. In a large bowl, combine the cake mix, melted butter, and eggs. Mix on low with an electric mixer.
4. Roll into 1-inch balls and roll in the powdered sugar/cornstarch mixture.
5. Place balls 2-inches apart on the prepared baking sheet.
6. Bake for 9-11 minutes or until set.
7. Let cool on the baking sheets for 5 minutes before transferring to a wire rack to cool completely.

peppermint Meltaway cookies

Makes about 3 dozen

What you need:

- 1 cup butter, at room temperature
- 1/2 cup powdered sugar
- 1/2 tsp peppermint extract
- 1 1/4 cup all-purpose flour
- 1/2 cup cornstarch
- 2 tbsp butter, softened
- 1 1/2 cups powdered sugar
- 2 tbsp milk
- 1/4 tsp peppermint extract
- 1/2 cup crushed soft peppermints

What to do:

1. Line 2 baking sheets with parchment paper and preheat your oven to 350 degrees F.
2. In a mixing bowl, cream together 1 cup of butter and 1/2 cup powdered sugar until fluffy.
3. Add in the peppermint extract.
4. In a separate bowl, mix together the flour and cornstarch and gradually add it to the butter/sugar mixture and mix well, making a dough.

5. Shape the dough into 1-inch balls. Place them 2 inches apart on the prepared baking sheets.
6. Bake for 10-12 minutes or until the bottoms are light brown.
7. Let the cookies cool on the baking sheets for 5 minutes then transfer to a wire rack to cool completely.
8. In a small bowl, beat 2 tbsp butter, 1 1/2 cups powdered sugar, 2 tbsp milk, and 1/4 tsp peppermint extract. Mix until smooth, making the icing.
9. Spread the icing over the cooled cookies and sprinkle with crushed peppermints.

Snicker Doodles

Makes 2 dozen

What you need:

- 1/2 cup shortening
- 3/4 cup granulated sugar
- 1 egg
- 1 tbsp vanilla
- 1 1/2 cups all-purpose flour
- 1/2 tsp baking soda
- 1/4 tsp cream of tartar
- 1 tbsp cinnamon
- 3 tbsp granulated sugar

What to do:

1. Preheat your oven to 350 degrees F and line a baking sheet with parchment paper.
2. Cream together the shortening and sugar in a mixing bowl with an electric mixer.
3. Add the egg and vanilla and mix well.
4. In a separate bowl, combine the flour, baking soda, salt, and cream of tartar and mix well.
5. Slowly add the dry ingredients to the wet ingredients.
6. Roll the dough into 1-inch balls.
7. In a small bowl, mix together 1 tbsp of cinnamon and 3 tbsp of sugar.
8. Roll the dough balls into the cinnamon and sugar mixture.

9. Place the balls on the prepared baking sheet and bake for 9-11 minutes or until edges are golden.
10. Let cool on the baking sheet for 5 minutes before transferring to a wire rack to cool completely.

sugar cookies

Makes 40-50 cookies

What you need:

- 1 cup unsalted butter, at room temperature
- 1 1/4 cup sugar
- 1 egg
- 1 1/2 tsp vanilla extract
- 1/2 tsp almond extract
- 3 cups flour
- 1 1/2 tsp baking powder
- 1/4 tsp salt
- Colored sugar, sprinkles, or icing-for decorating

What to do:

1. In a large mixing bowl, cream together the butter and sugar until fluffy.
2. Add in the egg, vanilla extract, and almond extract until well combined.
3. In a separate bowl, combine the flour, baking powder, and salt.
4. Slowly add the flour mixture to the butter/sugar mixture and mix well.
5. Roll the dough with a rolling pin between 2 sheets of parchment or wax paper and place on a baking sheet.
6. Refrigerate for 30 minutes.

7. Preheat your oven to 350 degrees F and line 2 baking sheets with parchment paper.
8. Cut the dough into shapes using cookie cutter and transfer to a baking sheet.
9. Sprinkle with colored sugars (if using) and bake for 8-12 minutes.
10. Cool on the baking sheet for 5 minutes then transfer to a rack to cool completely.
11. Store in an airtight container.

Turtle Brownies

Servings: 8-10

What you need:

- Your favorite brownie box mix plus ingredients the directions call for
- 1 tbsp strongly brewed coffee, leftover cold coffee is fine
- 8-oz caramel sauce
- 1 cup chopped pecans
- 1/2 cup chocolate chips
- 1/2 cup chopped pecans

What to do:

1. Preheat your oven to 350 degrees F and line an 8-inch square pan with aluminum foil. Let the foil hang over the edges a bit. Spray with non-stick spray.
2. Mix together your boxed brownie mix according to package directions.
3. Add the coffee, caramel sauce, 1 cup of chopped pecans, and chocolate chips to the mix and stir together.
4. Evenly sprinkle the 1/2 cup chopped pecans over the batter.
5. Bake for 22-25 minutes, or until a toothpick inserted into the center comes out clean.
6. Allow the brownies to cool, then cut them into squares and serve.

White Chocolate Cherry Cookies

Makes about 50 cookies

What you need:

- 1/2 cup maraschino cherries, drained and chopped
- 2 1/2 cups all-purpose flour
- 1/2 cup sugar
- 1 cup butter
- 12-oz white chocolate baking squares, finely chopped
- 1/2 tsp almond extract
- 2 drops red food coloring
- Sugar
- 2 tsp shortening
- Red and white sprinkles

What to do:

1. Preheat your oven to 325 degrees F and line a baking sheet with parchment paper.
2. In a large bowl, stir together the flour and 1/2 cup sugar. Cut in the butter until the mixture is crumby.
3. Stir in the cherries and 4-oz of white chocolate.
4. Stir in the almond extract and food coloring.
5. Form the mixture into a ball and knead until smooth.
6. Shape the dough into 1-inch balls and place them 2 inches apart on the prepared sheet. Flatten the balls.

7. Bake for 10-12 minutes then let cool on the baking sheet for 2 minutes.

White Chocolate Cranberry Cookies

Makes about 2 dozen

What you need:

- 3/4 cup unsalted butter, at room temperature
- 3/4 cup brown sugar
- 1/4 cup granulated sugar
- 1 large egg, at room temperature
- 2 tbsp vanilla extract
- 2 cups all-purpose flour
- 2 tsp cornstarch
- 1 tsp baking soda
- 1/2 tsp salt
- 3/4 cup white chocolate chips
- 1/4 cup dried cranberries

What to do:

1. In a large mixing bowl, beat the butter, brown sugar, and granulated sugar with a mixer until smooth and creamy.
2. Add the egg and vanilla and mix together.
3. In a separate bowl, stir together the flour, cornstarch, baking soda, and salt.
4. Slowly mix the flour mixture into the wet mixture until well combined.
5. Stir in the white chocolate chips and dried cranberries.

6. Chill the dough for at least 2 hours.
7. Preheat your oven to 350 degrees F and line a large baking sheet or two with parchment paper.
8. Roll the dough into 1-inch balls and place on the baking sheet(s) 1-2 inches apart.
9. Bake for 8-10 minutes or until golden around the edges.
10. Allow the cookie to cool on the sheet for 5 minutes then transfer to a wire rack to cool.
11. Serve or store in an airtight container.

TREATS AND CANDIES

candied pecans

Servings: 16

What you need:

- 1 cup sugar
- 3/4 cup brown sugar
- 1 1/2 tbsp cinnamon
- 1 egg white
- 2 tsp vanilla
- 4 cups pecans
- 1/4 cup water

What to do:

1. In a large bowl, mix together the sugar, brown sugar, and cinnamon.
2. In a separate bowl, whisk together the egg white and vanilla until it is a little bit frothy.
3. Spray your slow cooker with cooking spray.
4. Put the pecans in the slow cooker.
5. Pour the egg mixture over the pecans and stir well.
6. Sprinkle the cinnamon sugar mixture over the pecans and stir well.
7. Cover and cook on low for 3 hours, stirring every 30 minutes.
8. When there are 30 minutes left, pour 1/4 cup water into the slow cooker and stuff.
9. Spread the pecans on a baking pan and let them cool for 15-20 minutes.

candy caramels

Makes 48 pieces

What you need:

- 6-oz chocolate flavor candy coating, chopped
- 6-oz vanilla flavor candy coating, chopped
- 1 cup toffee pieces, crushed
- Christmas colored sprinkles.
- 48 decorative toothpicks
- 14-oz package of caramels, unwrapped
- 2-oz chocolate candy coating, chopped

What to do:

1. In a microwave safe glass bowl, place the 6-oz chocolate and 6-oz vanilla and microwave for 3 minutes, stirring every 30 seconds.

2. Place the toffee pieces and Christmas colored sprinkles in a shallow dish.
3. Insert a toothpick into each caramel piece.
4. Dip each caramel piece into the melted chocolate and vanilla mixture.
5. Coat each dipped caramel into the toffee and sprinkle mixture.
6. Place the coated pieces onto a sheet of wax paper and let cool before serving.

candy cane Marshmallow pops

Makes 36

What you need:

- 1 bag large marshmallows
- 1 large bag mini candy canes
- 1 large block of chocolate
- Crushed candy canes

What to do:

1. You can adjust this recipe to make whatever amount of servings you want!
2. Stick a mini candy cane into each large marshmallow.
3. Melt the chocolate in the microwave or over a double boiler.
4. Dip each marshmallow into the chocolate.
5. Roll each chocolate dipped marshmallow in the crushed candy canes.
6. Place on wax paper to dry.

Peppermint Dipped Oreos

Servings: 10-12

What you need:

- 1 package Oreos
- 1 package vanilla candy melts
- 1 package peppermint baking chips
- Crushed soft peppermints

What to do:

1. In a microwave safe bowl, combine the vanilla candy melts and the peppermint baking chips for 3 minutes, stirring every 30 seconds.
2. Dip each Oreo into the melted mixture then sprinkle with crushed peppermints.
3. Let cool on a sheet of wax paper before serving.

caramel marshmallow popcorn

Servings: 16

What you need:

- · 1 bag popped popcorn
- · 1/2 cup butter
- · 1 cup brown sugar
- · 1 tbsp corn syrup
- · 20 large marshmallows

What to do:

1. Pour the popped popcorn into a large bowl and remove any unpopped kernels.
2. Melt the butter in a large pot over medium heat.
3. Add the brown sugar and corn syrup into the melted butter.
4. Add the marshmallows and stir constantly on low heat until melted.
5. Pour the mixture over the popcorn and stir well.
6. Spread onto parchment paper and let cool.
7. Cut into squares before serving.

Cherry Cordials

Makes: 30

What you need:

- 10-oz Maraschino cherries
- 1 tbsp butter, softened
- 1 tsp corn syrup
- Warm water*
- 1 tbsp juice from maraschino cherry jar
- 1 1/2 cups powdered sugar
- 12-oz semi-sweet chocolate chips

What to do:

1. Line a baking sheet with paper towels and remove the cherries from the jar and place them on the baking sheet. Remove the stems if they have them.
2. Line another baking sheet with parchment paper.
3. In a mixing bowl, add the powdered sugar. Add 1 tbsp of warm water to it until it is dissolved. Add as little water as possible.
4. When the powdered sugar is just barely dissolved, add the softened butter, corn syrup, and 1 tbsp juice from cherry jar.**
5. Form this mixture into 1/2-inch balls and flatten them.
6. Place a cherry in the middle of each flattened ball and wrap the cherry up. Place each ball on the prepared baking sheet.
7. Place the baking sheet in the freezer for 30 minutes to 1 hour.

8. Melt the chocolate in a microwave safe bowl for about 3 minutes or until melted and smooth, stirring every 30 seconds.
9. Dip the balls in the chocolate using a fork or toothpick. Shake off the excess chocolate and return each ball to the baking sheet.
10. Refrigerate for at least 30 minutes on the baking sheet.
11. Serve or store in an airtight container.

*The original recipe calls for 1/2 tsp Invertase, which is an enzyme used in candy making and it helps to dissolve sugar. I couldn't find it at good old trusty Walmart so I just used water.

**If you happen to have or can find some Invertase, mix it in with the butter, corn syrup, and cherry juice; then add the powdered sugar.

Chocolate Peppermint Patties

Makes 8 dozen

What you need:

- 1-lb powdered sugar
- 4-oz cream cheese, softened
- 1/2 tsp peppermint extract
- 6-oz chocolate chips

What to do:

1. In a large mixing bowl, whip the cream cheese with an electric mixer.
2. Gradually add the powdered sugar and mix on low until it is all incorporated.
3. Add in the peppermint extract and mix well.
4. Roll the dough into teaspoon sized balls and place on a baking sheet lined with wax paper or parchment paper.
5. Make a small well in the center of each ball.
6. Cover the baking pan(s) and refrigerate for at least 2 hours.
7. Melt the chocolate chips in the microwave at 30 second intervals until melted and smooth, stirring between every interval.
8. Fill a piping bag or a freezer bag with a tiny piece of one corner cut off with the melted chocolate.

9. Fill each peppermint well with chocolate and let cool before serving.

Christmas Cookie Bark

Servings: 16-18

What you need:

- 14 Christmas Oreos, broken into pieces
- 1 1/2 cups pretzels, broken into pieces
- 1 cup Christmas colored M&M's
- 1-lb white chocolate or almond bark
- Christmas colored sprinkles

What to do:

1. Line a baking sheet with parchment paper.
2. Mix together the Oreo pieces, pretzels, and 3/4 cup of the M&M's.
3. Melt the white chocolate or bark in a microwave safe bowl for 2-3 minutes, stirring every 30 seconds until completely melted.
4. Drizzle the melted chocolate over the mixture on the baking sheet.
5. Top the chocolate with the rest of the M&M's and sprinkles.
6. Allow the bark to cool before breaking up and serving.

christmas crack

Servings: 10-12

What you need:

- Saltine crackers
- 1 stick of butter
- 1 cup brown sugar
- 1 tsp vanilla extract
- 1 bag of milk chocolate chips

What to do:

1. Preheat your oven to 400 degrees F.
2. Line a baking sheet with aluminum foil and spray with cooking spray.
3. Cover the cookie sheet with one layer of saltine crackers.
4. In a saucepan over medium heat, bring the butter and brown sugar to a boil while constantly stirring for 3 minutes.
5. Remove the saucepan from the heat and add in the vanilla extract.
6. Pour the mixture over the crackers and bake for 5-6 minutes.
7. Remove the baking pan from the oven and immediately pour the bag of chocolate chips over the top.
8. Allow the chocolate chips to melt for a minute or two and then spread it out evenly.
9. Allow it to cool then break into pieces.

cinnamon pecans

Servings: 4-6

What you need:

- 1 1/4 cup sugar
- 1 1/4 cup brown sugar
- 2 tbsp cinnamon
- 1/8 tsp salt
- 1 egg white
- 2 tsp vanilla
- 3 cups pecans
- 1/4 cup water

What to do:

1. In a large bowl, mix together the sugar, brown sugar, cinnamon, and salt.
2. In a separate bowl, mix together the egg white and vanilla.
3. Add the pecans to the egg mixture and coat them thoroughly.
4. Add the cinnamon mixture to the pecans and stir until they are evenly coated.
5. Pour the pecan mixture into your crockpot and cook on low for 3-4 hours, stirring occasionally.

cinnamon sugar pecans

Servings: 12

What you need:

- · 1-lb pecan halves
- · 1 large egg white
- · 1 tbsp water
- · 1/2 tsp vanilla extract
- · 1 cup sugar
- · 1/2 tsp salt

What to do:

1. Preheat your oven to 250 degrees F.
2. Line a baking sheet with parchment paper.
3. In a large mixing bowl, whisk together the egg white and vanilla until frothy.
4. In another mixing bowl, whisk together the sugar, cinnamon, and salt.
5. Add the pecans to the egg white mixture and coat evenly.
6. Pour half of the sugar mixture over the coated pecans, stir well, and then add the other half of the sugar mixture.
7. Pour the coated pecans onto the prepared baking sheet in an even layer.
8. Bake for 1 hour, stirring every 20 minutes.
9. Allow the pecans to cool then store in an airtight container.

Slow Cooker Christmas crack

Servings: 10-12

What you need:

- 8-oz unsalted peanuts
- 8-oz salted peanuts
- 6-oz semi-sweet chocolate chips
- 6-oz milk chocolate chips
- 10-oz peanut butter chips
- 1-lb white almond bark

What to do:

1. Layer all ingredients in your slow cooker, with the peanuts on the bottom.
2. Cover and cook on low for 2 hours.
3. Stir well and let cook for another 30 minutes to 1 hour.
4. Stir again then spoon the mixture onto wax paper or parchment paper.
5. Let cool for at least 1 hour.

DiViNiTY

Servings: 24

What you need:

- 2 2/3 cups sugar
- 2/3 cup light corn syrup
- 2/3 cup water
- 2 egg whites
- 1 tsp vanilla

What to do:

1. In a heavy saucepan over medium heat, stir together the sugar, syrup, and water. Bring to a boil, without stirring, and continue boiling until a thermometer reaches 260 degrees F.
2. Beat the two egg whites until they are stiff and easily form peaks.
3. Pour the syrup mixture into the egg white mixture and beat well.
4. Add in the vanilla and beat well.
5. When the divinity loses its shine and begins to hold its shape, spoon drops of it onto parchment paper.
6. Store in an airtight container at room temperature.

Easy Peanut Brittle

Makes 1.5 lbs

What you need:

- · 1 cup sugar
- · 1/2 cup corn syrup
- · 1 cup peanuts
- · 1 tsp butter
- · 1 tsp vanilla extract
- · 1 tsp baking soda

What to do:

1. Line a baking sheet with parchment paper and spray with non-stick spray.
2. In a 2 quart glass bowl, combine the sugar and corn syrup. Microwave on high for 4 minutes.
3. Stir in the peanuts and microwave for another 3 and a half minutes.
4. Stir in butter and vanilla and microwave for another minute and a half.
5. Stir in the baking soda and mix well.
6. Pour the mixture onto the prepared baking sheet and spread it out in a thin layer.
7. Let it cool completely then break into pieces before serving.

Easy Toffee

Servings: 6

What you need:

- · 1 cup almonds
- · 1 cup butter, cubed
- · 1 cup sugar
- · 1/2 tsp vanilla extract
- · 1/4 tsp salt
- · 1 1/2 cups semi-sweet chocolate chips
- · 1/3 cup chopped pecans

What to do:

1. Preheat your oven to 350 degrees F.
2. Line a baking sheet with parchment paper.
3. Spread the almonds in an even layer on the prepared baking sheet. Toast the almonds in the oven for about 10 minutes then remove from the oven and set aside.
4. In a saucepan over medium heat, combine the butter, sugar, vanilla, and salt. Whisk constantly until the butter has melted and becomes slightly brown. This is the caramel mixture.
5. Immediately pour the caramel mixture over the toasted almonds.
6. Sprinkle the chocolate chips over the caramel.
7. Sprinkle the pecans over the chocolate chips.
8. Let cool completely and then break into pieces.

Hay Stacks

Makes 24

What you need:

- 1 cup butterscotch chips
- 1/2 cup peanut butter
- 1/2 cup peanuts
- 2 cups chow mein noodles

What to do:

1. Microwave the butterscotch chips and the peanut butter in a large microwave safe bowl for 2-3 minutes, stirring every 30 seconds.
2. Remove the bowl from the microwave and stir in the peanuts and the chow mein noodles.
3. Spoon dollops of the mixture onto wax paper or parchment paper. Let sit for 2-3 hours or until completely cooled and hardened.
4. Serve immediately or store in an airtight container.

Martha Washingtons

Makes 24

What you need:

- 2 cups shredded coconut
- 8 cups powdered sugar
- 1 stick butter, melted
- 1 can sweetened condensed milk
- 1 tsp vanilla
- 4 cups chopped pecans
- Chocolate almond bark

What to do:

1. Combine the coconut, powdered sugar, butter, sweetened condensed milk, vanilla, and pecans in a large bowl.
2. Roll the mixture into small balls and let them chill in the refrigerator for at least 30 minutes.
3. Melt the chocolate and dip the chilled balls into the chocolate, coating well.
4. Allow the chocolate covered balls to cool on parchment paper.

Oreo Balls

Servings: 24

What you need:

- 15.5-oz package of Oreos
- 8-oz of cream cheese, softened
- 3/4-lb vanilla almond bark, chopped
- Christmas colored sprinkles

What to do:

1. Line a baking sheet with parchment paper.
2. Place the Oreos in a food processor and pulse until finely chopped.
3. Place the chopped Oreos in a large bowl and add in the cream cheese. Mix well.
4. Roll the mixture into 24 balls and place on the prepared baking sheet.
5. Place the baking sheet into your refrigerator for at least 30 minutes or until the balls are firm.
6. In a microwave safe bowl, melt the almond bark in the microwave for 2 minutes, stirring every 30 seconds.
7. Place a skewer or toothpick into the Oreo balls and dip into the melted almond bark until coated.
8. Cover the balls with sprinkles and place back onto the baking sheet.
9. Let the balls cool for at least 30 minutes before serving.

oreo peppermint Bark

Servings: 15

What you need:

- 10 mini candy canes, crushed
- 12 Oreos, chopped
- 1 cup chocolate chips
- 1 1/2 cups white chocolate chips

What to do:

1. Line a baking sheet with parchment paper and spray with non-stick spray.
2. Add the milk chocolate chips to a microwave safe bowl and microwave for 30 second intervals until smooth and melted. Stir between every 30 second interval.
3. Pour the melted chocolate onto the prepared pan and spread it evenly.
4. Sprinkle the chopped Oreos on the warm chocolate and chill for 10 minutes.
5. Add the white chocolate to a microwave safe bowl and microwave for 30 second intervals until smooth and melted. Stir between every interval.
6. Pour the melted white chocolate over the Oreos and spread evenly.
7. Sprinkle the chopped candy canes over the warm white chocolate.
8. Chill until completely set then break into pieces.

peanut Butter Truffles

Makes 35-40

What you need:

- 16-oz Nutter Butter Cookies
- 8-oz cream cheese
- 8-oz Reese's Mini Peanut Butter Cups, quartered
- 12-oz milk chocolate chips
- 3/4 tbsp shortening
- Christmas colored sprinkles

What to do:

1. In a food processor, blend the Nutter Butters into fine crumbs.
2. Cube the cream cheese and place the cubes in the food processor and blend in with the Nutter Butter crumbs.
3. Transfer this mixture to a large bowl.
4. Fold the quartered Reese's cups into the mixture.
5. Roll the mixture into 1-inch balls and place on a sheet of parchment or wax paper on a baking sheet.
6. Freeze for about an hour.
7. Melt the chocolate chips and shortening in a microwave safe bowl in the microwave for 2-3 minutes, stirring every 30 seconds.
8. Dip the frozen balls into the melted chocolate.
9. Place the dipped balls back on the baking sheet to dry.
10. Add the sprinkles before the chocolate dries completely.

peppermint Bark

Servings: 12

What you need:

- 12-oz semi-sweet chocolate chips
- 12-oz white chocolate chips
- 1 tsp peppermint extract
- 1/2 cup crushed peppermints

What to do:

1. Line a baking sheet with parchment paper and spray with non-stick spray.
2. Place the semi-sweet chocolate chips in a microwave safe bowl for 2 minutes, stirring every 30 seconds.
3. Pour the melted chocolate onto the prepared pan and spread into an even layer. Let cool.
4. Repeat step 2 with the white chocolate chips then stir in the peppermint extract.
5. Spread this mixture onto the cooled chocolate layer on the baking sheet.
6. Sprinkle the crushed peppermints onto the white chocolate layer and gently press the pieces in with a spatula.
7. Let cool then break into pieces before serving.

peppermint patties

Servings: 12

What you need:

- 1/4 cup butter, softened
- 1/3 cup corn syrup
- 4 cups powdered sugar
- 1-2 tsp peppermint extract
- Green and red food coloring
- 12 cup sugar

What to do:

1. In a mixing bowl, combine the softened butter and the corn syrup.

2. Add the 2 cups of powdered sugar and peppermint extract and beat until fully combined.

3. Stir in another cup of powdered sugar.

4. Pour the mixture out onto a cutting board and sprinkle it with the last cup of powdered sugar.

5. Knead the mixture until smooth.

6. Divide the dough into 3 portions.

7. Color one portion with red food coloring and one with green food coloring. I made a well into each portion and filled the well with food coloring then folded and kneaded so it wasn't as messy.

8. Shape the portions into 3/4-inch balls and roll the balls in the sugar.
9. Flatten the balls with a fork.
10. Refrigerate for 3-4 hours before serving or place in an airtight container.

peppermint popcorn Bark

Servings: 18

What you need:

- 2 bags popped popcorn
- 6-oz of candy canes, crushed
- 1 package of white almond bark
- 1 tsp peppermint extract

What to do:

1. Place the popcorn in a very large bowl.
2. Pour the crushed candy canes on top of the popcorn.
3. Melt the almond bark according to the package instructions.
4. Add the peppermint extract to the melted almond bark and stir well.
5. Pour the melted almond bark over the popcorn and stir until the popcorn is coated.
6. Pour the coated popcorn onto wax paper and spread in an even layer.
7. Allow the popcorn to harden then break it into pieces.

Peppermint Puppy Chow

Servings: 10-12

What you need:

- 6-7 cups Chex cereal
- 2 cups white chocolate chips
- 1 tsp vegetable oil
- 1 3/4 cups crushed candy canes
- Powdered sugar

What to do:

1. Place the cereal in a large bowl.
2. In a microwave safe bowl, microwave the white chocolate chips and vegetable oil at 30 seconds intervals until melted and smooth. Stir between each interval.
3. Pour the melted chocolate over the cereal and stir to coat well.
4. Pour the mixture into a large ziplock bag.
5. Place the crushed candy canes and about 2 cups of powdered sugar in the bag. Close the bag and shake well to coat. Add more powdered sugar if you want!

peppermint Rice krispie Treats

Servings: 10-12

What you need:

- 10 1/2-oz bag of peppermint mini marshmallows
- 1/4 cup butter
- 5 cups rice krispie cereal
- 1/4 cup semi-sweet chocolate chips
- 1/4 cup white chocolate chips
- 1/2 tsp vegetable oil
- 1/8 tsp peppermint extract
- 3 medium sized candy canes, crushed

What to do:

1. Line a 9x13-inch pan with foil and spray with non-stick spray.
2. Melt the butter in a large bowl in the microwave.
3. Add the marshmallows to the bowl and stir well.
4. Heat at 30 seconds intervals until the marshmallows are melted and smooth. Stir between each interval.
5. Add the Rice Krispies to the bowl and stir to combine.
6. Press the mixture into the prepared pan.
7. In a microwave safe bowl, combine the white chocolate chips and 1/4 tsp vegetable oil. Heat in the microwave until melted and smooth, stirring every 30 seconds.

8. Sprinkle the melted white chocolate over the rice krispie treats.
9. In a microwave safe bowl, combine the semi-sweet chocolate chips, 1/4 tsp vegetable oil, and the peppermint extract. Microwave until melted and smooth, stirring every 30 seconds.
10. Drizzle the chocolate over the Rice Krispies.
11. Sprinkle the crushed candy canes on top and let sit until the chocolate is set before cutting into squares and serving.

peppermint sticks

Makes 16

What you need:

- 4-oz semisweet chocolate chips
- 1 tsp shortening
- 2/3 cup toasted pecans, chopped
- 16 3-inch soft peppermint sticks

What to do:

1. In a small saucepan over low heat, combine the chocolate chips and shortening. Cook until melted.

2. Transfer the melted chocolate to a bowl.
3. Place the pecans in a shallow dish.
4. Dip each peppermint stick into the melted chocolate then coat with crushed pecans.
5. Place on wax paper and let cool.

Reindeer Chow

Servings: 16-18

What you need:

- 14 cups Chex cereal
- 18-oz red and green M&M's
- 12-oz semi-sweet chocolate chips
- 1/2 cup butter
- 1 cup peanut butter
- 1 tsp vanilla extract
- 4-5 cups powdered sugar

What to do:

1. In a microwave safe bowl, melt the peanut butter and butter at 30 second intervals until butter is melted completely.
2. Add the chocolate and stir until they are melted, microwave at 30 second intervals if necessary.
3. Pour half of the Chex cereal into a very large bowl.
4. Drizzle half of the chocolate/peanut butter mixture over the cereal and mix with a spoon.
5. Pour 1 cup of powdered sugar into a gallon zip lock bag and add half of the covered cereal mix. Close the bag and shake until the cereal is coated.
6. Repeat step 5 until all of the coated cereal is covered in powdered sugar.
7. Repeat steps 3-6 until all cereal is covered in powdered sugar.

8. Place all of the cereal in a large container and toss in the M&M's.

Rolo Turtles

Makes 50

What you need:

- 50 checkerboard pretzels
- 50 individual Rolos
- 50 pecan halves, toasted

What to do:

1. Preheat your oven to 350 degrees F.
2. Line a baking sheet with parchment paper.
3. Evenly space the pretzels on the prepared baking sheet.
4. Place one Rolo on each pretzel.
5. Place the baking sheet in the preheated oven for 5 minutes.
6. Remove the baking sheet from the oven and place a pecan on top of each Rolo and carefully press down. Don't burn yourself!

Snowballs

Makes 64

What you need:

- 12-oz white chocolate chips
- 1/4 cup heavy cream
- 1 1/4 cup slivered almonds, finely ground
- 2 tbsp dark rum
- 1 1/2 cups shredded coconut

What to do:

1. In a double boiler, melt the white chocolate chips with the heavy cream, stirring constantly.
2. Stir in the almonds and the rum.
3. Pour the mixture into a square baking pan and chill for an hour or until firm.
4. Cut into squares and roll each square into a ball.
5. Roll each ball into the coconut.
6. Chill until ready to serve.

CAKES, PIES, AND DESSERTS

Bread Pudding

Servings: 4-6

What you need:

- 10 slices raisin cinnamon swirl bread, cut into cubes
- 1 14-oz can sweetened condensed milk
- 1 cup water
- 1 tsp vanilla
- 5 eggs, beaten

What to do:

1. Place the bread cubes into your slow cooker.
2. Mix the sweetened condensed milk, water, vanilla, and eggs together in a bowl and pour the mixture over the bread.
3. Stir to coat the bread evenly.
4. Cook on low for 3-4 hours or until set.

Apple Crisp

Servings: 4

What you need:

- 5 large apples; peeled, cored, and sliced
- 1 tsp nutmeg
- 1 tsp cinnamon
- 1 tbsp maple syrup
- 1 tbsp lemon juice
- 1 cup oats
- 1/2 cup brown sugar
- 1/2 cup all-purpose flour
- 4 tbsp butter
- 1/4 tsp salt

What to do:

1. Add the sliced apples, half the nutmeg, half the cinnamon, maple syrup, and lemon juice to your slow cooker and mix together well.
2. In a mixing bowl, mix together the oats, butter, sugar, flour, the other half the nutmeg, the other half of cinnamon. Spread this mixture over the apples in the slow cooker.
3. Cook on low for 4 hours before serving.

Gingerbread Pudding

Servings: 8-10

What you need:

- · 1 14-oz package of gingerbread mix
- · 1/2 cup milk
- · 1/2 cup raisins
- · 2 1/4 cups water
- · 1 cup packed brown sugar
- · 3/4 cup butter

What to do:

1. Coat your slow cooker with non-stick cooking spray.
2. In a medium bowl, combine the gingerbread mix and milk. Stir in the raisins. Spread the mixture into your slow cooker.
3. In a saucepan over medium-high heat, combine the water, brown sugar, and butter. Bring to a boil, reduce heat, and simmer for 5 minutes.
4. Pour the sugar mixture over the batter in the slow cooker.
5. Cook for 2 hours.
6. Turn off the slow cooker and let it sit for 1 hour without the lid.
7. Serve with vanilla ice cream.

MoNkeY BreAd

Servings: 10

What you need:

- 1 16-oz roll of refrigerated biscuits
- 1/2 cup sugar
- 1/2 cup brown sugar
- 1 tsp cinnamon
- 1 stick butter, melted
- 4-oz cream cheese, cubed and softened

What to do:

1. Spray the inside of your slow cooker with non-stick spray.
2. Combine the sugar, brown sugar, and cinnamon in a gallon zip lock bag and set aside.
3. Cut each biscuit into 6 pieces.
4. Dip each biscuit piece into the melted butter.
5. Place dipped biscuits into the gallon zip lock bag with the sugar mixture and shake well to coat.
6. Pour any remaining butter into your slow cooker.
7. Transfer all biscuit pieces to your slow cooker.
8. Cook on low for 2-3 hours or until dough is done.
9. Stir in cubed cream cheese before serving.

Pumpkin Bars

Servings: 8-10

What you need:

- 2 cups flour
- 2 tsp baking powder
- 2 tsp cinnamon
- 1/2 tsp nutmeg
- 1 tsp salt
- 1 tsp baking soda
- 4 eggs
- 1 2/3 cup sugar
- 1 cup oil
- 1 15-oz can pumpkin
- 8-oz cream cheese, softened
- 1/3 cup butter
- 3 cups powdered sugar
- 1 cup whipped cream
- 1 tbsp milk

What to do:

1. Preheat your oven to 350 degrees F and grease a 15x10 baking pan.
2. In a small bowl, sift together the flour, baking powder, cinnamon, nutmeg, salt, and baking soda.
3. In a large mixing bowl, combine the eggs, sugar, oil, and pumpkin until mixed well.

4. Gradually mix in the dry ingredients and mix well.
5. Spread the batter into the baking dish and bake for 25-30 minutes or until a toothpick inserted into the center comes out clean.
6. While the bars are in the oven, place the cream cheese and butter in a mixing bowl and cream together.
7. Add in the powdered sugar, whipped cream, vanilla extract, and milk. Mix until fluffy.
8. Place the frosting in the refrigerator.
9. When the bars are finished cooking, let them cool completely then frost them generously.

carrot cake

Servings: 8-10

What you need:

- 1 cup sugar
- 2 eggs
- 1/4 cup water
- 1/3 cup vegetable oil
- 1 1/2 cups flour
- 1 tsp vanilla
- 1 tsp baking powder
- 1/2 tsp baking soda
- 1 tsp cinnamon
- 1 cup packed grated carrots
- Cream cheese frosting

What to do:

1. In a mixing bowl, cream the sugar, eggs, water and oil. Add the flour, vanilla, baking powder, baking soda, and cinnamon. Blend until combined. Stir in the carrots by hand.
2. Spray the inside of your slow cooker with non-stick cooking spray.
3. Pour the batter into your slow cooker and spread it evenly.
4. Cook for 2-3 hours on low or until a toothpick inserted into the middle comes out clean.
5. Remove the cake from the slow cooker, let it cool, and top it with cream cheese frosting.

Frozen Peppermint Pie

Servings: 16

What you need:

- 2 premade Oreo cookie pie crusts
- 8-oz whipped cream, thawed
- 1.5 quart container of peppermint ice cream
- Crushed candy canes
- 8 Oreos, crushed

What to do:

1. Soften the ice cream until it can be easily mixed.
2. Mix the ice cream and whipped cream.
3. Spread the mixture into the two pie crusts.
4. Freeze for several hours then top with crushed candy canes and crushed Oreos.

Pumpkin Pie

Servings: 6

What you need:

- 1 15-oz can of pumpkin
- 2/3 cup cinnamon bun flavored coffee creamer
- 2 tbsp pumpkin pie spice (divided)
- 1 9-oz yellow cake mix
- 1 cup chopped pecans
- 1/4 cup butter

What to do:

1. Spray the inside of your slow cooker with non-stick spray.
2. In a medium bowl, mix together the pumpkin, coffee creamer, and 1 tbsp of pumpkin pie spice.
3. Spread the mixture into your slow cooker.
4. In a separate bowl, mix together the cake mix, pecans, and 1 tsp pumpkin pie spice.
5. Sprinkle the mixture over the pumpkin mixture in your slow cooker.
6. Drizzle the melted butter over the top of the dry mixture.
7. Cover and cook on high for 2 1/2 hours.
8. Serve warm.

YOU WILL ALSO ENJOY

WWW.HANNIEPSCOTT.COM/BOOKS

ABOUT THE AUTHOR

Hannie P. Scott, Full-Time Mom and Food Blogger

Driven by her desire for cooking for others (and herself), Hannie spends a lot of time in the kitchen! She enjoys sharing her love of food with the world by creating "no-nonsense" recipe books that anyone can use to make delicious meals.

Hannie attended the University of Southern Mississippi and received a Bachelor's degree in Nutrition & Dietetics. She enjoys cooking and experimenting with food. She hopes to inspire readers and help them build confidence in their cooking. All Hannie's recipes are easy-to-prepare with easy-to-acquire ingredients.

For more recipes, cooking tips, and Hannie's blog, visit:

www.HanniePScott.com

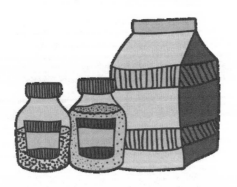

NOTES

NOTES

NOTES

NOTES

NOTES

NOTES